D0315188

MY FIRST ENCYCLOPEDIA

An eye-catching series of information books designed to encourage young children to find out more about the world around them. Each one is carefully prepared by a subject specialist with the help of experienced writers and educational advisers.

KINGFISHER
Kingfisher Publications Plc
New Penderel House, 283-288 High Holborn, London WC1V 7HZ

First published in paperback by Kingfisher Publications Plc 1994
2 4 6 8 10 9 7 5 3 1
1BP/0500/SF/((FR)/135MA

Originally published in hardback under the series title Young World
This edition © copyright Kingfisher Publications Plc 2000
Text & Illustrations © copyright Kingfisher Publications Plc 1992

ISBN 1 85697 262 3

Phototypeset by Waveney Typesetters, Norwich
Printed in China

MY FIRST ENCYCLOPEDIA

On the Move

Kingfisher

Series consultant and author
Brian Williams

Educational consultant
Daphne Ingram

Editor
Sian Hardy

Designer
Robert Wheeler

Illustrators
Peter Dennis (pages 12-13, 52-53, 96-97)
Andrew French (pages 66-67, 70-71, 74-75)
Tony Gibbons and Lawrie Taylor (pages 64-65, 68-69,
72, 80-81, 92-93 *bottom*, 100-101)
David McAllister (pages 82-83, 86-87, 90-91, 92-93 *top*)
Industrial Art (pages 78-79)
Oxford Illustrators (pages 14-17, 22-23, 26-27, 34-35,
38-41, 44-49, 54-59, 73, 98-99, 102-119)
Vincent Wakerley (pages 20-21, 24-25, 28-31,
36-37, 42-43, 50-51, 84-85, 88-89)

About this book

Whenever you catch a bus or a plane, ride in a car or on a bicycle, you are using a form of transport.

Transport means carrying things and people from place to place. Early forms of transport were slow. Today, journeys that used to take days, or even weeks, take only a few hours. A jet aeroplane can fly round the world in just one and a half days.

Because transport has become faster, easier and cheaper, our world and the way we live have changed. Our cities have airports. Roads, tunnels and bridges criss-cross the countryside. People often travel to faraway places, and our shops are filled with goods from all over the world. We depend on transport.

People around the world travel in many different ways. In some countries people drive on the right-hand side of the road. In others they drive on the left. In this book we have shown a mixture of left- and right-hand drive, as well as a selection of number plates from different countries.

CONTENTS

ALL KINDS OF TRANSPORT

WHEELING ALONG

FOUR WHEELS MORE WHEELS

WHEELS ON RAILS

OCEAN TRANSPORT

INTO THE AIR

THE SPACE AGE

All kinds of

transport

✸ A busy street

This busy street is full of people on the move. A truck delivers fish that has come from far away to a fishmonger. A bus take people to work or school. All around us ar cars, trucks and motorbikes carrying peop and things from one place to another.

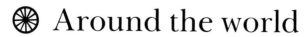

⊛ Around the world

So much of the food we eat every day come
from faraway places. Have you ever
thought how it reaches us?

Roads and railways join cities that are
hundreds of kilometres apart. Big
container ships bring us food from countri
across the sea.

anes travel faster than ships or trains or
ucks. A big jet can fly around the world in
ily one and a half days. Some planes
irry cargo, but most are used to carry
issengers. Rockets can now even carry
ople into Space.

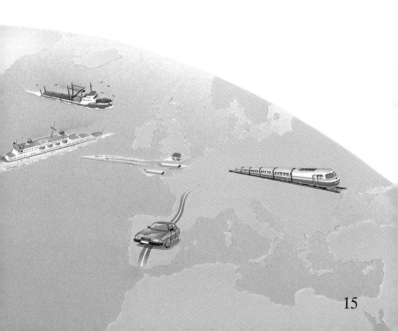

⊛ Animal power

People cannot always use cars and trains to move around. In some places it would be too difficult to build a road or a railway.

Camels can walk for days across a hot desert. Most cars would sink into the sand. In the jungle, the easiest way to get around is often to take a canoe down the river.

'hen this happens, people often use
iimals to help them carry their heavy
ads from place to place.

gh up in the mountains of Peru, people use
mas to carry their loads. In Lapland, the
ipps use reindeer to pull their sledges across
e snowy ground.

Amazing facts

✺ The wheel was the first important transport invention. People first made wheels over 5,000 years ago. They made them by fastening pieces of wood together

✺ The world's longest highway is the Pan-American Highway. It is over 24,000 kilometres long, although there is a gap in the middle. It starts in Alaska in the far north of North America and ends in Brazi in South America.

✺ The biggest car park in the world is in Edmonton, in Canada. It has parking spaces for 30,000 cars.

Wheeling

along

🏍️ A bicycle

On a bicycle you use your feet to move the pedals. Follow the numbers to find out what happens next.

rear light helps other people see you

3. The back wheel pushes the bike forwards.

sadd

pec

2. The chain turns the back wheel.

1. The pedal turn the chai

chain

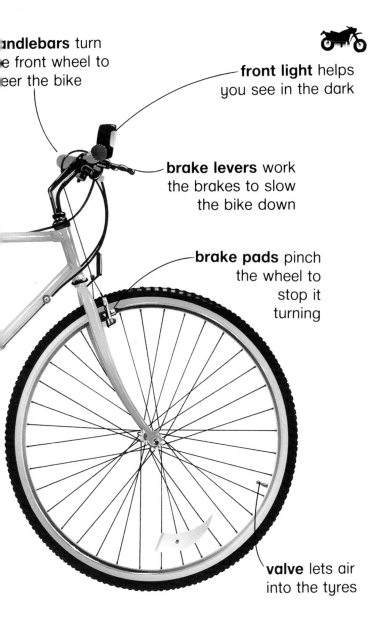

andlebars turn
e front wheel to
eer the bike

front light helps
you see in the dark

brake levers work
the brakes to slow
the bike down

brake pads pinch
the wheel to
stop it
turning

valve lets air
into the tyres

21

🏍 Safety on a bike

Riding a bike is fun, but always remember: safety first! Check your bike regularly and take it to a repair shop if anything is wrong. You should learn your highway code befor cycling on the road. The picture shows you eight things you need for your bike.

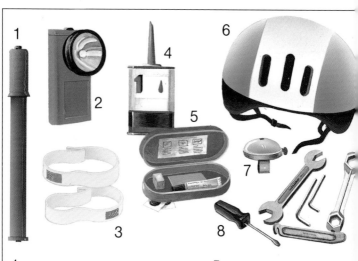

1 pump

2 light

3 reflector bands

4 oil can

5 puncture repair kit

6 helmet

7 bell

8 tool kit

...ake sure the brake pads have not worn
...own and always keep your chain well oiled.

...ou may need help to mend
...puncture. First find
...e hole in the inner
...be, and then cover
...with a patch.

🏍 Early bikes

People have enjoyed riding on two wheels ever since bicycles were first invented.

The hobbyhorse was an early bike with no pedals. You pushed yourself along with your feet.

Later bikes, like the vélocipède, had pedals fixed to the front wheel.

Because of its big front wheel, the penny-farthing could go very fast. But it was difficult to ride.

One, two, three wheels

A one-wheeled cycle is called a
unicycle, and a three-wheeled cycle
is called a tricycle.

Could you balance
on a unicycle?

This racing tandem
is built for two
people. The
front rider
steers the bike.

In some Asian cities,
pedal-powered rickshaws
are used as taxis.

🏍 A motorbike

A motorbike is powered by a petrol engine. The engine drives a shaft or a chain that turns the back wheel. The back wheel pushes the motorbike forwards.

brake light shows other drivers the bike is slowing down

shock absorbers cushion the rider from bumps in the road

waste gases from the engine escape through the **exhaust pipe**

rror

speedometer shows how fast the bike is going

brake lever

tank holds petrol to fuel the engine

headlight

indicator

petrol engine

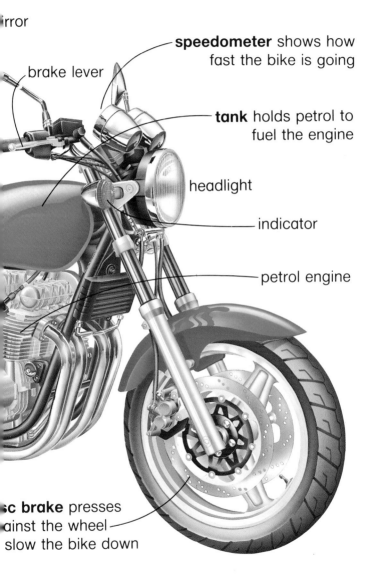

sc brake presses ainst the wheel slow the bike down

🏍 Working bikes

The police use fast motorbikes. Unlike car
which need lots more space, motorbikes ar
not held up in traffic jams. So a police
motorcyclist can quickly reach an accident
and call for help by radio.

⚝ All kinds of bikes

opeds have smaller
gines than motorbikes
d so are less
werful.

The Harley Davidson is a
powerful American
motorbike. Its
engine is bigger
than the engine
of a small car.

sidecar fixed to the
le of a motorbike
n carry an extra
ssenger.

🏍 Racing bikes

People enjoy racing pedal bikes and
motorbikes. They race on tracks and on
roads. Racers use bikes that are faster than
ordinary bikes.

The Tour de France
is the most famous
pedal bike race.
The race is in
stages and lasts
about three weeks.

motocross races, riders
ramble their bikes over
umps and through streams.

rag bikes only race along a short track, but they
ach speeds of over 300 kilometres an hour in a
w seconds.

rand Prix
cers speed
ound a winding
ick. The riders
in into the bends to
ep their balance.

Amazing facts

Air-filled bicycle tyres were invented by John Dunlop about 60 years after the first bicycle appeared. Before that, bicycle wheels had metal or wooden rims. This made them very uncomfortable to ride.

The Tour de France is the longest bicycle road race. It covers more than 3,000 kilometres in total, but is broken into stages.

The fastest speed on a motorbike is over 512 kilometres an hour. This record was set by Donald A. Vesco in 1978 on a bike with two engines.

A 'wheelie' means riding on the back wheel only. The record for a wheelie on a motorbike is an amazing 331 kilometres non-stop.

Four wheels

more wheels

A car has hundreds of parts. It has a strong metal frame, called a chassis, and a body made of thin metal panels. Follow the numbers to see how it works.

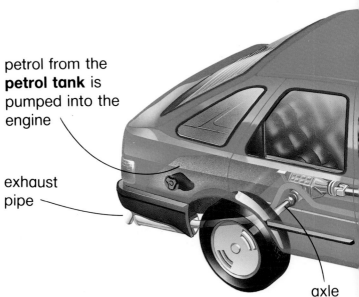

petrol from the **petrol tank** is pumped into the engine

exhaust pipe

axle

5. The back wheels push the car forwards.
In some cars the engine turns the front wheels. This is called front-wheel drive.

4. The propeller sho turns the axle and t turns the back whee

34

Turning the key
arts the engine.

2. Petrol in the engine is mixed with air. Electric sparks make the mixture explode over and over again, pushing pistons up and down.

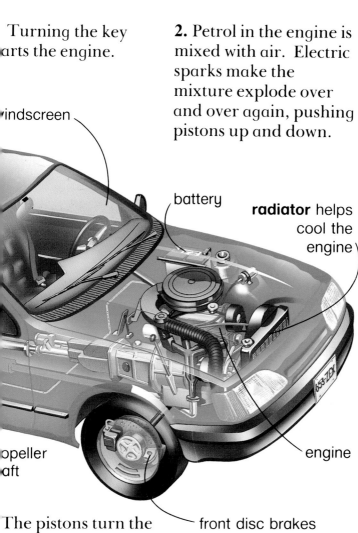

indscreen

battery

radiator helps
cool the
engine

opeller
aft

engine

The pistons turn the
opeller shaft.

front disc brakes

◼️ Big cars, small cars

Cars come in many shapes and sizes. Peop
use them for all kinds of different jobs.

This car has big whee
for driving acro
rough groun

Cars with powerful
engines can tow heavy
loads.

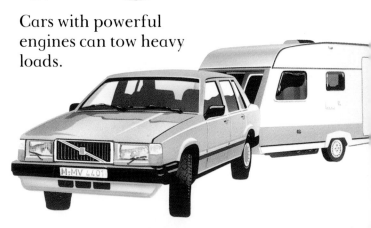

A sports car has a lo
low shape. This he
it go fo

n estate car has lots of room to store luggage in.
roof rack can be useful too.

Taxis carry people
around towns
and cities.

small car is easier to
rk in a busy street
an a big car.

Motoring then and now

When cars were first invented, motoring was a real adventure. The cars often broke down and there were no proper roads. People wore goggles to keep dust out of their eyes and coats to keep them warm.

Motoring is very different today. Modern cars are fast and comfortable and roads and motorways criss-cross the countryside. But there are so many cars that they cause traffic jams and pollute the air with their exhausts.

🚛 At the garage

Like all machines, cars need looking after.

Without petrol the car will not go. The oil in the engine should be checked regularly. The air pressure in the tyres should also be checked from time to time. Keeping a car clean helps protect it against rust.

t the garage, mechanics service and repair
rs. They check the engine, brakes and
her parts and replace them if they have
orn out. They can raise the car on a ramp
work underneath it.

🚛 Racing cars

Racing cars are built to go much faster than ordinary cars. During a race, they can reach speeds of nearly 400 kilometres an hour. Air rushing over the aerofoils at the front and back of the car pushes the car downwards to help keep the wheels on the track.

the weather is dry, racing cars use tyres called
cks. These have no tread, or pattern, cut in
em. If the race track is wet, they use treaded
res, which give a better grip on the track.

Buses and coaches

The first buses were pulled by horses. Late[r]
there were buses on rails, called trams.
Today most buses have diesel-oil engines.

This brightly coloured
bus is used in Pakistan.
When the bus is full,
people sit on
the roof.

This Lond[on]
double-decker b[us]
can carry mo[re]
than 70 peopl[e]

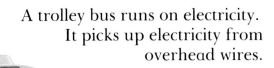

A trolley bus runs on electricity.
It picks up electricity from
overhead wires.

An articulated bus is
extra long. The bus
can bend at the join
to go round corners.

Coaches take people
on long-distance
journeys.

An articulated truck

trailer carries the load

trailer hook fits into the fifth wheel to link the trailer and the tractor unit

fifth wheel

diesel oil for the engine is carried in the **fuel tank**

n articulated truck is made up of two
arts: a trailer and a tractor unit. The trailer
like a big container. It has no engine and
pulled along by the tractor unit. Because
a articulated truck is made up of two
arts, it can go round tight corners.

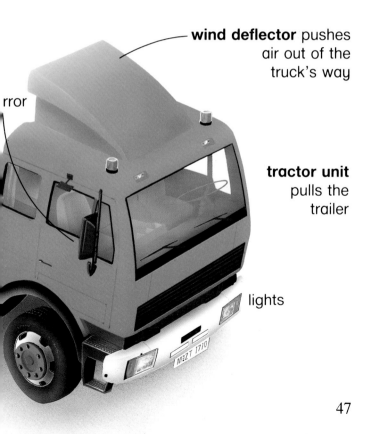

wind deflector pushes
air out of the
truck's way

rror

tractor unit
pulls the
trailer

lights

47

 The truck driver

At a busy warehouse, a forklift truck loads the trailer. Once everything is in place, the driver can set off. On a long trip, he may be away from home for a week or more.

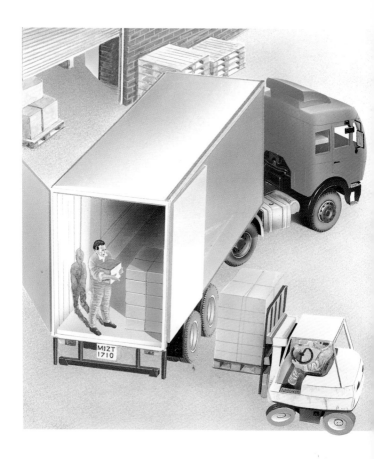

truck driver keeps in touch with other
ivers using a telephone in the cab. A jack
mes in useful if he has to change a wheel.
fter a hard day's driving, the driver climbs
to his bunk bed at the back of the cab. At
e end of the journey, he hands over his
elivery papers and the trailer is unloaded.

Special trucks

Trucks are designed and built for the different jobs they do.

A tanker carries petrol, gas or chemicals inside a strong metal tank.

The trailer of a refrigerated truck is cold inside, like a fridge or freezer, so that it can keep food fresh.

car transporter carries new cars from the
ctory to the showroom.

his logging truck has
crane to lift logs on
the trailer.

A roadtrain is a truck
that pulls three or
more trailers. It is
used on very long
journeys.

Emergency!

Fire! Cars and cyclists make way for the emergency vehicles as they speed through the streets. Firemen are soon at work putting out the fire. Policemen keep peopl away from the danger area. The ambulance arrives in case anyone is hurt.

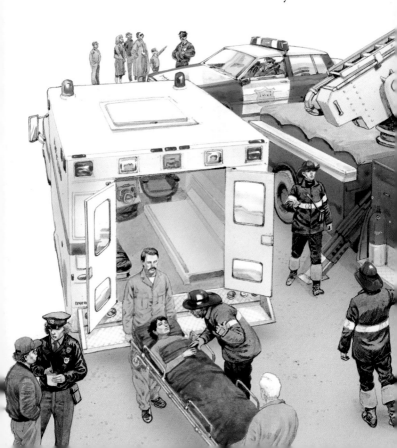

![] Off the road

The farm tractor has a powerful engine
and big back wheels. The deep tread, or
pattern, on the tyres helps them grip the
mud when the tractor is pulling a heavy
plough up and down a field.

The big tyres on this all-terrain vehicle help
travel over rough ground. It can climb
eep hills and splash through mud and
ater. To steer, the driver uses handlebars
stead of a steering wheel.

A mobile crane

The mobile crane can travel on roads like any truck. But at the building site, it puts down metal legs, called stabilizers, that rais it off the ground and keep it steady as it lifts its heavy load.

Pulley wheels wind the load up and down on wires.

The driver pulls levers inside the cab to work the crane's arm, or boom.

stabilizers

The boom can be made longer or shorter, like a telescope.

boom

57

Building a road

First, planners make maps to show where the new road will go. They work out how much traffic will use the road. Then, huge machines get to work building the road.

1. Bulldozers clear away piles of rocks and earth.

2. Machines called scrapers level the ground to make it flat.

dumper
truck

3. Dumper trucks carry away the waste soil and deliver a mixture of crushed stones called hardcore. This is pressed into the earth to make a firm base for the road. Graders then smooth the surface of the road ready for the top layer.

roller

4. A paving machine spreads a layer of tarmac on the road. Tarmac is a mixture of small stones and tar. Finally, a roller presses the tarmac down to make it smooth and hard.

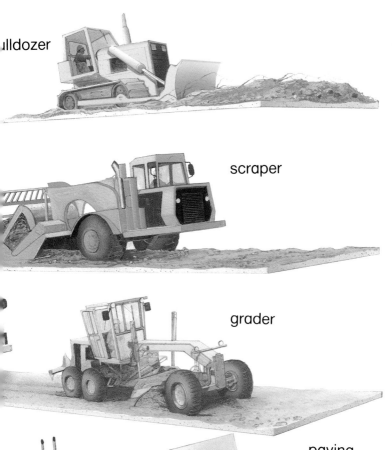

ulldozer

scraper

grader

paving
machine

59

![truck] Bridges and tunnels

Bridges and tunnels shorten journeys.
A bridge can carry railway tracks across a
river, or take cars safely over another road.
Tunnels allow us to go through mountains,
beneath city streets and under rivers.

o build a tunnel, engineers must bore rough rock under the ground. If the rock hard, machines drill holes for explosives at will blast the rock away.

the rock is softer, a machine called a nnel-boring machine is used. This has a tting face that bites away the rock. The nnel is then lined with steel and concrete.

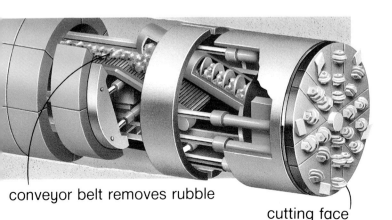

conveyor belt removes rubble

cutting face

Amazing facts

There are more than 500 million cars in the world. About one third of them are driven in North America.

The biggest land vehicles are two giant crawlers used to carry space rockets to the launch pad at Cape Canaveral in the United States of America. Each is as big as a twelve-storey building.

The world's fastest passenger car is the Jaguar XJ220. It can go at over 340 kilometres an hour.

The fastest land vehicle in the world is *Thrust 2*. This car has jet engines and can travel at over 1,019 kilometres an hour.

The Saint Gotthard Tunnel is the world's longest road tunnel. It is 16 kilometres long and burrows beneath the Alps in Switzerland.

Wheels

on rails

At the station

Trains start and end their journeys at statio
Stations are busy places, with people
hurrying to catch their trains. Indicator
boards show passengers which platform to
go to and what time the train will depart.

Trains come and go all day long. A fast
express train may be taking passengers to a
city hundreds of kilometres away. Slower
trains bring people to work in the city.
Trains carry letters and parcels too.

🚂 A high-speed train

This French TGV is the world's quickest passenger train. (In French, TGV stands for High-Speed Train.) The TGV travels at speeds of up to 300 kilometres an hour. Its streamlined shape helps it to go fast.

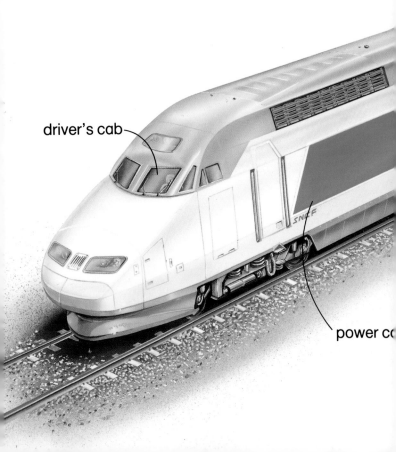

driver's cab

power c

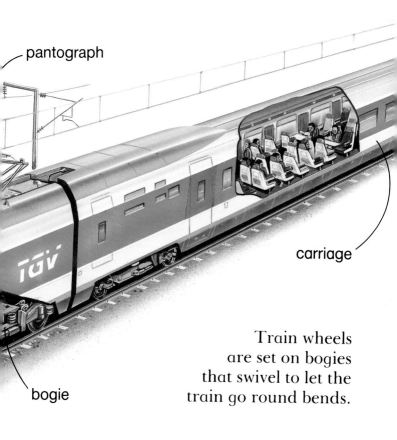

pantograph

carriage

Train wheels
are set on bogies
that swivel to let the
train go round bends.

bogie

he TGV is powered by electricity. It picks
) electricity from an overhead wire with a
ding arm called a pantograph. Motors in
e power cars use this electricity to drive
e wheels and pull the carriages along.

🚂 Driving a train

Inside the driver's cab on a TGV there is a computer that tells the driver how fast he can go and when to slow down and stop. The driver controls the speed of the train with the wheel in front of him.

rain wheels have no tyres. Instead they
ave a rim to stop them slipping off the rail.
a train wants to turn left or right, it must
ove on to a different track. Movable
acks, called points, switch the train from
ne track to another. The points are
ntrolled electronically from a signal box.

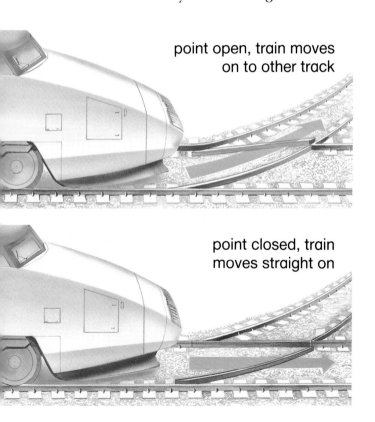

point open, train moves
on to other track

point closed, train
moves straight on

A steam train

Steam trains burn wood and coal to heat water and make steam. The steam then pushes pistons that turn the wheels.

This steam train travelled across North America over 100 years ago. The cowcatcher in front cleared the track.

Trains around the world

Steam trains are still used on some railways. This one is in India.

A modern diesel train burns oil to make electricity. The electricity drives the train's motors.

A rack and pinion train is designed to climb steep hills. It has an extra wheel with teeth that fit into notches on a third rail. This stops the train slipping down the hill.

third rail

🚂 Underground

Underground trains carry people through tunnels under busy city streets. The trains run on electric power. Passengers go down in lifts or on escalators to reach the platforms.

Overground

ike a train that runs underground, a
nging monorail can save space in a busy
ty. Monorail means the train travels on
st one rail. A hanging monorail, such as
e one shown above, hangs below the rail.
sturdy arm holds it in place. Other
onorails sit on the rail.

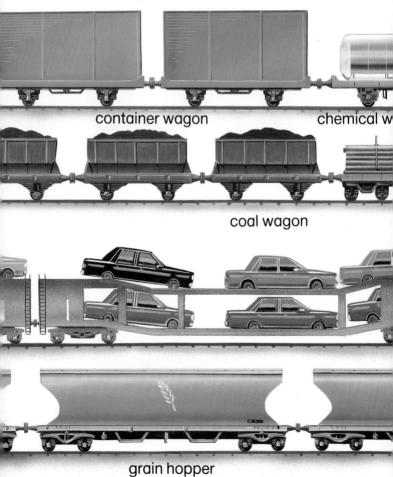 Freight trains

As well as carrying passengers, trains also transport all kinds of goods, called freight, from one city to another.

container wagon

chemical w

coal wagon

grain hopper

reight trains can be made up of as many as
0 different wagons. They are linked
gether in a freight yard.

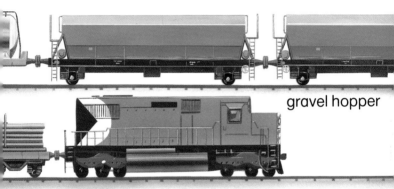

gravel hopper

tcar

car carrier

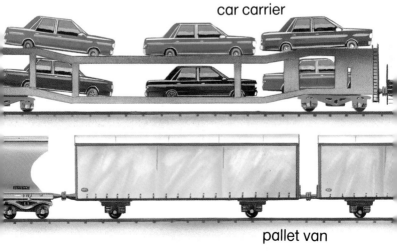

pallet van

Amazing facts

The first public steam railway was the Stockton and Darlington Railway, in England. In 1825 a train made up of 33 carriages carried the first passengers at a top speed of 24 kilometres an hour.

The first underground railway opened in London in 1863. To begin with, the trains were pulled by steam locomotives, so the tunnels were always full of smoke.

The speed record for a train is 515 kilometres an hour. This was set by a French TGV in 1990. New trains that are being developed, called Maglev trains, could go even faster. Maglev trains float above the track and are pushed along by magnets.

The longest railway in the world is over 9,400 kilometres long and runs from Moscow to Nakhodka, in Russia.

Ocean

transport

A port

At a port, ships are loaded and unloaded. Tugs guide big ships to their parking place called berths. Huge cranes lift cargo off the ships to be stored in warehouses. To keep the water deep, dredgers scoop up mud from the bottom.

ferry

warehou

dredger

crane

An ocean liner

An ocean liner is like a floating hotel. The passengers enjoy their journey in comfort. They can swim, play games on deck, or watch a film while the crew run the ship.

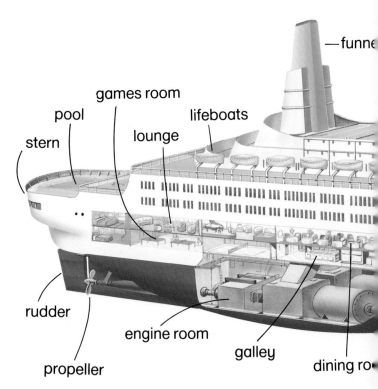

funnel

games room

pool

lifeboats

stern

lounge

rudder

engine room

galley

propeller

dining room

he parts of a ship all have names. The
dy is called the hull. The front is called
e bow and the back is called the stern.
drooms are called cabins and the kitchen
called the galley. The captain controls the
ip from the bridge.

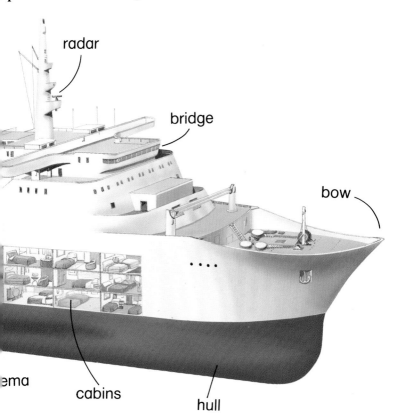

radar

bridge

bow

ema

cabins

hull

lighthouse

buoy

buoy

Taking a liner in and out of port can be difficult. Usually, a pilot who knows the port well takes control of the ship. Floating buoys show the pilot where the channels of deep water are. The flashing light on a lighthouse warns ships of dangerous rocks.

avigation means finding the way. Once
e ship is out on the open sea, the captain
id crew on the bridge work out the ship's
urse using maps. They use radar to spot
her ships, and satellite signals to check
eir position.

The engine room

Down in the hull are the ship's engines.
Some ships have diesel engines, others have
gas turbine engines. The engines turn the
propeller and this drives the ship through
the water. The rudder steers the ship.

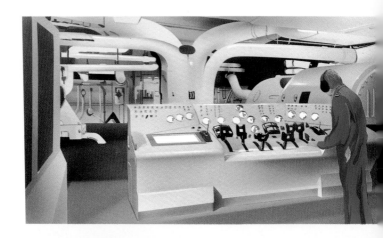

rudder

propeller

How a ship floats

he weight of a ship's hull pushes it down
to the water. But the water tries to get
ick and pushes up against the hull. If the
o pushes are equal, the ship floats. But if
e ship is made too heavy, it will sink.

arks on the ship's side,
lled the Plimsoll line,
ow how low down in the
ter the ship can safely go.

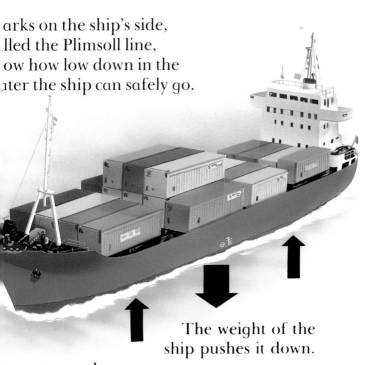

The weight of the
ship pushes it down.

e water pushes
against the hull.

All kinds of ships

Ships come in different shapes and sizes.

A hydrofoil skims over the
surface of the sea. It has
underwater 'wings' that
lift it out
of the
water.

Hovercraft float on a cushion
of air. Fans blow air
downwards and lift the
hovercraft off the water.

Paddle steamers travel up
and down rivers.
They are
driven by a
big wheel at
the stern.

Lifeboats rescue people at
sea. They are small, but
they are almost
unsinkable.

Fishing trawlers have a
winding engine at the
stern to haul in
their heavy nets.

Supertankers carry oil
in huge tanks. They
are the biggest ships
in the world.

Canals

Canals are waterways built by people.
When a canal runs through land that is on
slope, it must be built in a series of steps. T
move up and down these steps, canal boats
have to go through locks.

his canal boat is going up a step. Once the
oat is in the lock, the gates are closed.
hen water is slowly let into the lock. When
e water has risen to the correct level, the
ites open and the canal boat moves on.

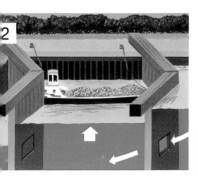

Sailing ships

Sailing ships are powered by the wind pushin
against the sails. Sailing ships like this one
carried people and cargo over 100 years ago
But people stopped using big sailing ships
when faster steamships were invented.

The junk is
a Chinese
sailing ship.

This racing yacht can go very
fast. The big sail at the front is
called a spinnaker.

A catamaran has two
hulls. Most sailing
boats have only one.

A submarine

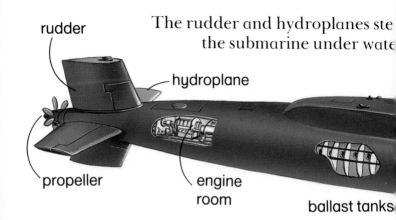

rudder

hydroplane

propeller

engine room

ballast tanks

The rudder and hydroplanes ste
the submarine under wate

Submarines are ships that go under water.
They can stay under water for weeks
without coming to the surface. The
commander controls the submarine from
the control room. By raising the periscope
he can look around above the water.

ballast tanks are
flooded with water

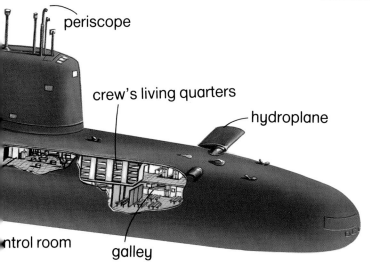

periscope

crew's living quarters

hydroplane

ntrol room

galley

> dive, the submarine's ballast tanks are
>oded with seawater. The submarine sinks.
> come back up to the surface, air is blown
to the ballast tanks, pushing out the water.

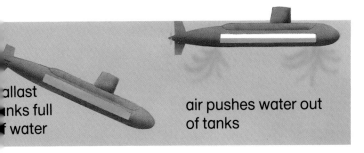

allast
nks full
f water

air pushes water out
of tanks

Amazing facts

The first expedition to sail around the world was led by the explorer Ferdinand Magellan in 1519. The voyage took nearly three years and proved that the Earth is round, and not flat as many people had believed.

Over a hundred years ago, the fastest sailing ships were clipper ships. A clipper could cross the Atlantic in 12 days. The fastest crossing by a modern passenger liner is three and a half days.

The world's biggest ship is an oil tanker *Hellas Fos*, of 555,051 tonnes. The largest passenger ship is the cruise liner *Norway*, which is 315 metres long.

Famous shipwrecks include the English warship *Mary Rose* and the liner *Titanic*. The *Mary Rose* sank when it turned over in 1545 and the *Titanic* hit an iceberg in 1912.

Into

the air

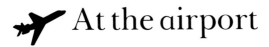 # At the airport

An airport needs lots of space. There are long runways, hangars for aircraft that nee servicing and repairs, and terminal buildings where the passengers check in.

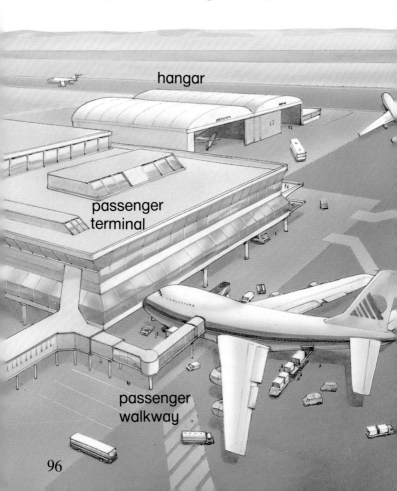

hangar

passenger terminal

passenger walkway

efore the passengers board their plane, it
ust be cleaned and refuelled. Food is taken
board and the baggage is stored in the
old. When everything is ready, the plane
oves to the end of the runway to wait for
ermission to take off.

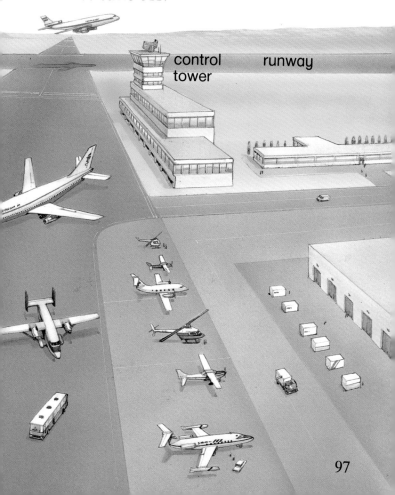

control tower

runway

✈ A jumbo jet

This Boeing 747 is the world's biggest passenger plane. It has room for about 400 passengers. Its four turbofan engines push it through the air at over 900 kilometres an hour. It has a wide body, called the fuselage, thin strong wings and a big tailfin.

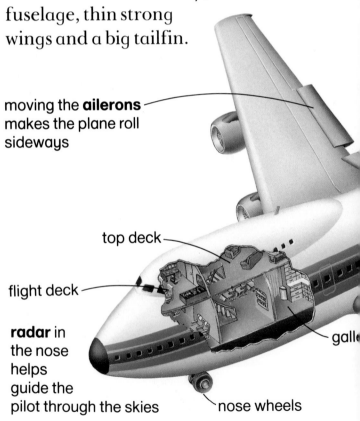

moving the **ailerons** makes the plane roll sideways

top deck

flight deck

radar in the nose helps guide the pilot through the skies

gall

nose wheels

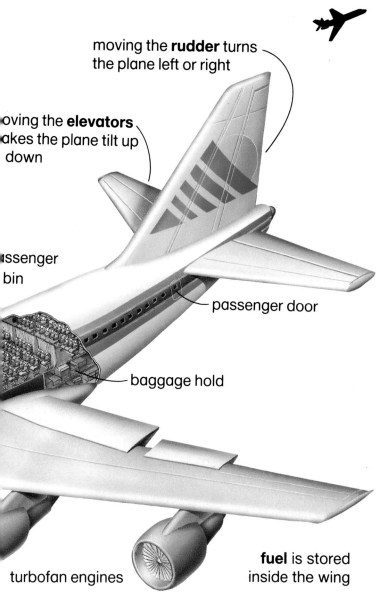

moving the **rudder** turns the plane left or right

oving the **elevators** akes the plane tilt up down

ssenger bin

passenger door

baggage hold

turbofan engines

fuel is stored inside the wing

99

✈ Catching a plane

When passengers arrive at the airport, they check their baggage in at the airline desk. they are travelling abroad, they must then go through passport control.

loading the pla

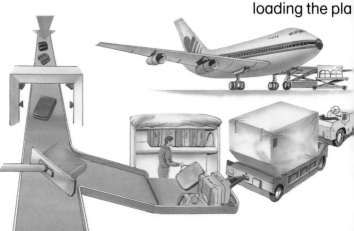

hile passengers wait to board the plane, aggage handlers load their baggage into e plane's hold. During the flight, the abin crew look after the passengers. They rve drinks and meals. Once the plane has nded, the passengers collect their baggage.

loading the plane

Permission to take off

The pilot waits for the controllers in the
control tower to give him permission to tak
off. The controllers use radar to keep trac
of all the planes in the air or on the ground

omputers on the flight deck help the pilot
ontrol the plane. They show him how high
he plane is flying and how fast it is going.
ven if the computers break down, the pilot
an still fly the plane using instruments such
s the altimeter and the artificial horizon.

altimeter

artificial
horizon

✈ How a plane flies

As the engines drive the plane along the runway, air flows around the wings. The faster the plane goes, the faster the air flows

The forward push that comes from the engines is called thrust.

The upward push is called lift.

Air flowing over an under the curve wings creates li

he wings of a plane have a curved shape.
'hen air flows over and under the wings,
creates an upward push on the plane. As
e plane picks up speed, the upward push
ts stronger. When it is strong enough, it
ts the plane off the ground.

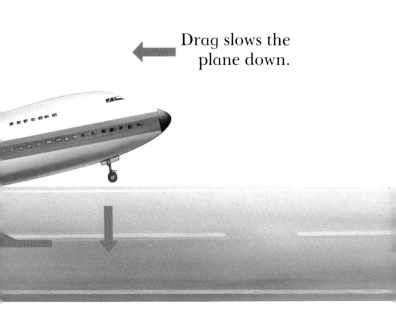

Drag slows the
plane down.

The weight of the
plane pulls it
downwards.

✈ All kinds of aircraft

Any flying machine is an aircraft. Aircraft
can be huge or tiny. Some can fly faster
than others, but each has a job to do.

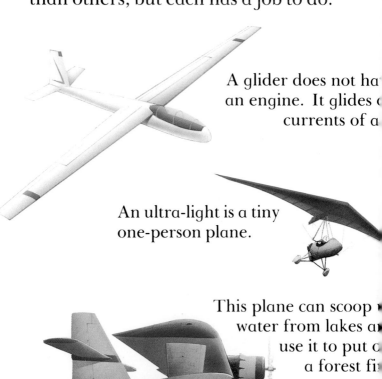

A glider does not ha[ve]
an engine. It glides [on]
currents of a[ir]

An ultra-light is a tiny
one-person plane.

This plane can scoop [up]
water from lakes a[nd]
use it to put o[ut]
a forest fi[re]

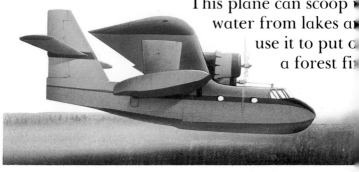

oncorde is the only supersonic
rliner in the world. It is
personic because it can
y faster than the
eed of sound.

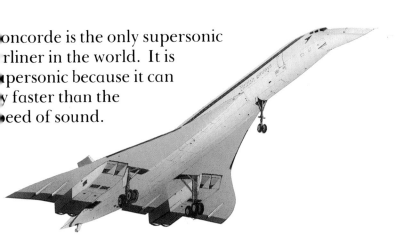

his small commuter jet
rries people on
siness trips.

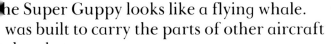

he Super Guppy looks like a flying whale.
 was built to carry the parts of other aircraft
d rockets.

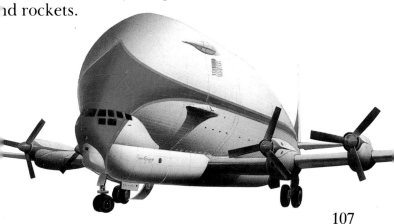

 Old planes

The first pilots were brave and skilful.
Their planes were small and slow, but they
made history in the air.

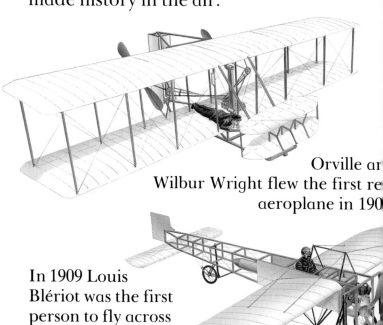

Orville an
Wilbur Wright flew the first re
aeroplane in 190

In 1909 Louis
Blériot was the first
person to fly across
the sea from France
to England.

In 1927 Charles Lindbergh v
the first pilot to fly acr
the Atlantic Ocean alo

Military planes

ir forces and navies use special planes.
ome are very fast fighters and bombers.
ome, such as the Harrier jump jet, do not
ed a long runway. They can land in a
eld or on the deck of a ship.

Hornet

Mirage

Harrier

✈ Helicopters

A helicopter has spinning rotor blades instead of wings. It can fly upwards or downwards or sideways and can even hover in mid-air.

To move the helicopter in all these different directions, the pilot changes the angle of the rotor blades using a joy stick and foot pedals.

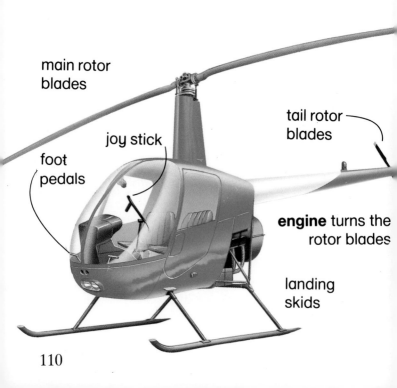

main rotor blades

tail rotor blades

joy stick

foot pedals

engine turns the rotor blades

landing skids

elicopters are often used to rescue people
sea. The pilot keeps the helicopter steady
ile one of the crew is lowered on a line to
lp the person in the water. Then both can
winched up to safety.

Amazing facts

In 1933 Wiley Post was the first person to fly solo around the world. His journey was 25,000 kilometres long and took him 7 days, 18 hours and 49 minutes.

In 1986 a plane flew non-stop around the world without refuelling. Two pilots were squashed inside the small cabin for 9 days, 3 minutes and 44 seconds.

The world's heaviest aircraft is the Russian An-225 Dream. It weighs 508 tonnes.

The fastest aircraft of all time was the American X-15A-2, a rocket plane that reached 7,274 kilometres an hour in 1967.

The Harrier jump jet is a V/STOL plane. This means that it can fly straight ι or down. The letters V/STOL stand for Vertical/Short Take Off and Landing.

The

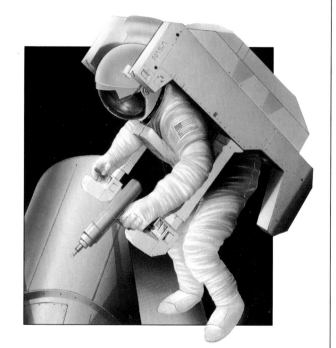

Space Age

Lift off

It takes five engines, burning 20 tonnes of fuel a second, to lift the space shuttle off the launch pad. The shuttle can carry up to seven astronauts into Space. It can also carry satellites and a laboratory in its large payload bay.

main
fuel ta

payload bay

booster rockets give extra power during launch

About two minutes after lift off, the two
booster rockets fall away from the shuttle
and parachute into the sea.

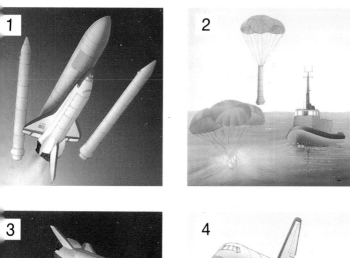

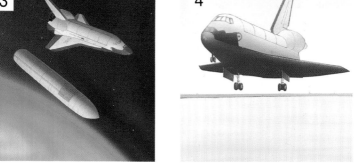

A few minutes later, the main fuel tank also
falls away. Once its mission is over, the
shuttle returns to Earth and lands on a
runway like an aeroplane.

# On board the shuttle

The living area and the flight deck are in the nose of the shuttle. In the middle is the payload bay. Once the shuttle is out in Space, the doors of the payload bay can open. On this mission the shuttle is carrying a telescope and a spacelab.

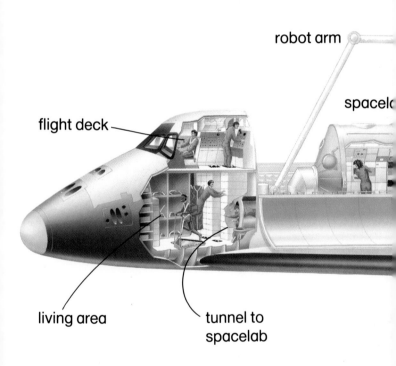

robot arm

spacel

flight deck

living area

tunnel to spacelab

he astronauts carry out scientific xperiments in the lab. One of the stronauts is working out in the ayload bay. He is attached to robot arm to stop him oating away.

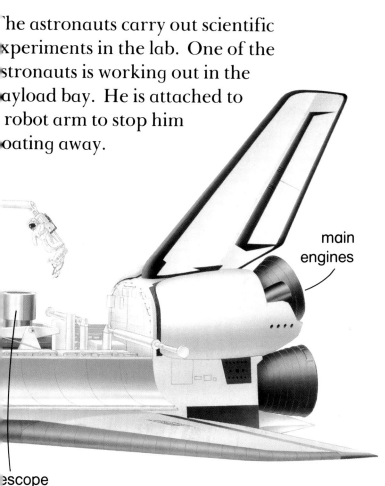

main engines

escope

small **thruster rockets** move the shuttle while it is in Space

Life in Space

In Space there is no gravity. So unless they are strapped down, the astronauts float about inside the shuttle. They even have to strap themselves on to the exercise machine and into their sleeping bags.

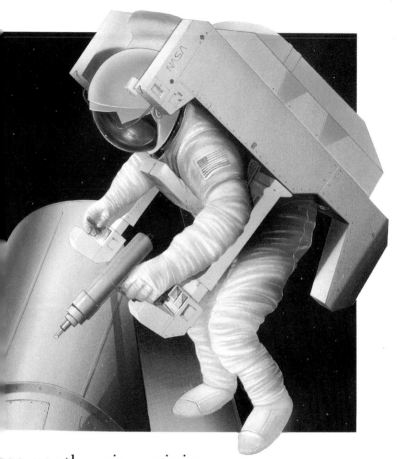

ecause there is no air in
pace, astronauts must wear a spacesuit
hen they are working outside the shuttle.
his astronaut is also wearing an MMU —
Man Manoeuvering Unit. By firing jets in
e MMU, the astronaut can move about.

Amazing facts

The Space Age began in 1957 when the USSR launched the first artificial satellite. It was called *Sputnik 1*.

The world's first human space traveller was Yuri Gagarin of the USSR. He travelled once around the Earth in 1961.

The first people to land on the Moon were the American astronauts Neil Armstrong and Edwin Aldrin. They landed in the *Apollo 11* spacecraft on 21 July, 1969.

In 1977 the Americans launched the *Voyager 2* robot spacecraft on a voyage of exploration. It sent back television pictures of four planets – Jupiter, Saturn, Uranus and Neptune – and is still travelling out in Space.

NDEX

121

The editor would like to thank Trans World
Airlines Inc. and the many other companies
and individuals who assisted in the
preparation of this book.

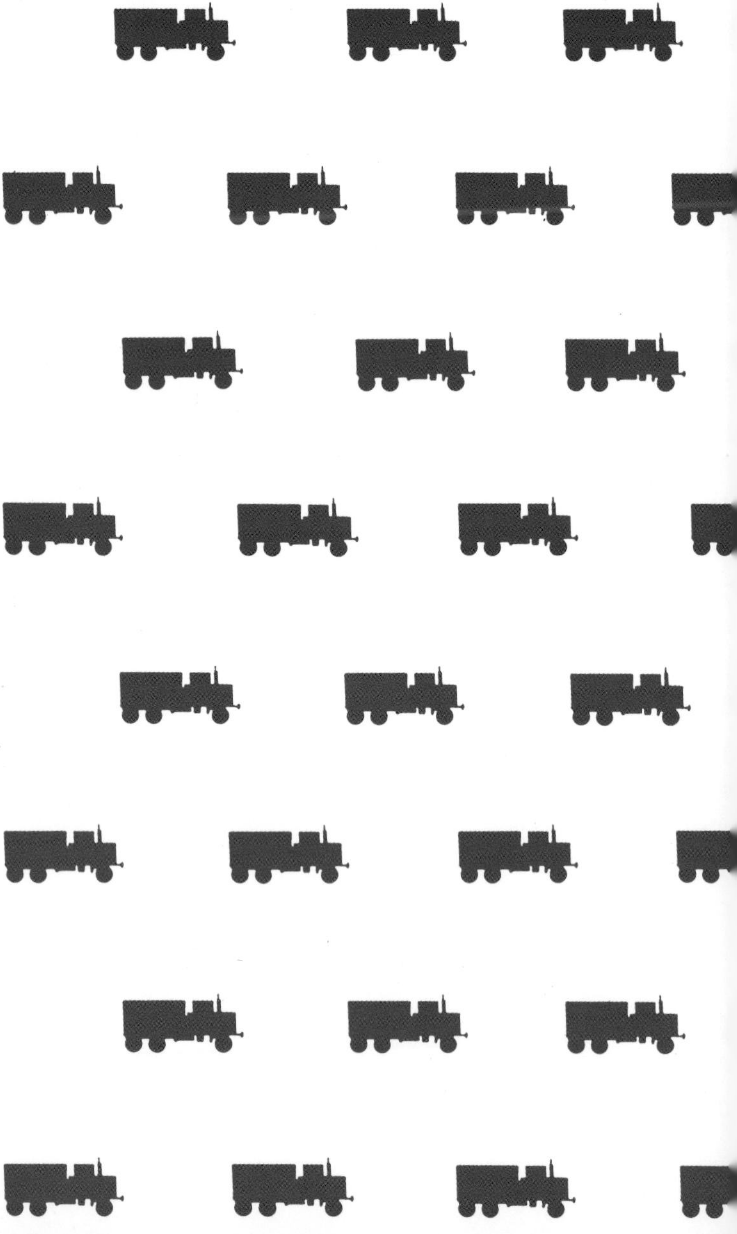